Little Lambs

Jonah and the Great Fish

by Karen Williamson

Illustrated by Sarah Conner

“Go to the city of Nineveh,” God said to Jonah. “Tell the people there to stop doing wrong!”

"That sounds very scary!" thought Jonah.
So he ran away.

Jonah got as far as the sea.

There he found
a boat.
He jumped
on board.

Soon Jonah was far away from Nineveh.
But God wasn't pleased with him.
He sent a great storm.

The boat rocked and rolled in the waves.

But Jonah lay below fast asleep.

The sailors came and woke Jonah.
"Pray to God to save us!" they shouted.

"Just throw me overboard," said Jonah.
"Then you'll be safe."

Whoooosh!
The sailors flung
Jonah into the sea.

At once the storm stopped.

But Jonah plunged deep,
deep into the sea.

Suddenly, with a gulp,
a great fish swallowed him.

Poor Jonah found he was sitting inside the fish's tummy.

He felt very frightened!

"I'm really sorry," Jonah prayed.

"If you save me, Lord,
I'll do everything you tell me!"

Three days later, the fish swam to shore.

Splatttttt!

The great fish spat Jonah out onto the wet sand.

Immediately Jonah ran off to Nineveh.

Now he wanted to do what God told him.

Jonah said to the people of Nineveh,
"God loves you. He wants you to obey him."